Contents

About the contributors

Romy Tiongco

Before joining Christian Aid, Romy worked in a mission parish and then as a full-time community-based development worker in the Philippines for 16 years. He co-founded an organisation called the 'Muslim-Christian Agency for Rural Development'. The agency has been a partner of Christian Aid since 1979. He now works with the Churches and Communities Department of Christian Aid and is based in the North West of England.

Myrna Bajo

Myrna Bajo has been working with indigenous people in the southern Philippines since 1974. She has also been involved in providing guidance and services to urban poor and Muslim women, the paralysed and post-polio victims. With two other colleagues in other parts of the country, she pioneered the training of Community-based Health Workers and broke the myth that health knowledge and skills are the monopoly of medical professionals. In 1988 she co-founded an organisation called Community Action for Rural Development (CARD) which has been a partner of Christian Aid since the mid-1990s.

Kate Fenn-Tye

Kate Fenn-Tye used to work in communications in the corporate sector and then for the Scottish Episcopal Church. She now spends most of her time caring for three children, as well as undertaking writing and editorial work on ecumenical projects. She is a member of Stirling Baptist Church.

Foreword

The season of Lent is traditionally a time for Christians to stop and consider their lives and what is going on around them. The period of prayer and fasting from Ash Wednesday until the great festival of Easter takes our focus away from ourselves and our needs, concentrating more on God and His plans for His world. 'Voices from the South' is a publication bringing new stories into our worldview, new challenges for those of us who are comfortable, and a new awareness of our part as the Body of Christ in the world today.

Exploring and studying the United Nations Millennium Goals would be a positive thing to do at any time. Christians are always aware that we can have an impact for good and there is much to study, much to reflect on and much to pray over in this guide. I warmly commend its use at any time of the year and hope that it inspires many to pray and act in the way prescribed by Scripture: to act justly, to love kindly and to walk humbly with our God.

Most Reverend Mario Joseph Conti,
Archbishop of Glasgow

Lent is a very precious season in the Christian year. It's a time when people often forge new friendships through studying together. 'Voices From the South' lets us extend these friendships onto the world stage and deepen our understanding of God's love for all people, all year round.

Dr Alison Elliot OBE
Moderator of the Church of Scotland

INTRODUCTION
Voices from the South

Then you shall call, and the Lord will answer;
you shall cry, and he will say, Here I am.

Isaiah 58: 9

'Voices from the South' contains stories of ordinary people in their ordinary lives. They were selected because they portray the struggle between the forces of death and the forces of life. Attitudes, behaviours, structures and systems that slowly but effectively cause death are making Jesus re-live his passion and death (see Matthew 26). Jesus is still suffering today. But where individuals and groups, church-based or of other faiths or orientation, in solidarity with the deprived and the oppressed, are planting the seeds of hope and fullness of life, the God who loves, the God who acts is there. May these voices from the South, the 'developing countries', lead us to hear and see where God's interventions to set his people free are happening in the world. God's liberating action cannot be confined to the churches. God is a free God and chooses his own instruments of salvation. But the churches have an added responsibility to provide a living witness to God's faithful, effective and redeeming love.

The arrival of the third millennium was welcomed with great hopes and dreams for the future by many in the churches. This study guide invites you to revisit these dreams by looking into some of the Millennium Development Goals set out by the United Nations. There are eight goals with 18 sub-targets and 48 indicators.

The Millennium Development Goals (MDG)

1. Eradicate extreme poverty and hunger
2. Achieve universal primary education
3. Promote gender equality and empower women
4. Reduce child mortality
5. Improve maternal health
6. Combat HIV/AIDS, malaria and other diseases
7. Ensure environmental sustainability
8. Develop a global partnership for development

A full critique of the MDG is beyond the scope of this project. Instead, during the five weeks of the study, participants are encouraged to consider where and how these goals may reflect the goal, or purpose, of Jesus (John 10:10) – 'I came that they may have life, and have it abundantly', and to join the never-ending journey of integrating life and faith - living and believing.

The importance of the five themes of poverty, education, health, trade and empowerment is reflected in Jesus' own mission and preoccupation with healing, teaching, concern for justice and for the poor and, of course, the freedom which can be found through redemption. In the synagogue in Nazareth Jesus said, quoting from Isaiah:

> 'The Spirit of the Lord is upon me, because he has anointed me
> to bring good news to the poor.
> He has sent me to proclaim release to the captives and recovery
> of sight to the blind,
> To let the oppressed go free, to proclaim the year of the Lord's
> favour'
> (Luke 4: 18, 19 and Isaiah 61: 1, 2)

Jesus went on to add, "today this scripture is fulfilled in your hearing" (Luke 4: 21). The challenge for us as Christians is how to emulate Jesus in his preoccupations, and translate them into action.

The first session focuses on poverty. The Marshall Plan succeeded in rebuilding the economies of Western Europe after the Second World War. Attention was then shifted to the so-called developing countries of the South. The 60s were named the 'Development Decade'. Since then governments, churches and non-government organisations have launched development strategies. In spite of all these attempts, poverty persists.

The guide does not look into the development strategies. It tries to dig into something completely different and hardly mentioned in development publications – if at all. It invites each participant and each study group to reflect on who we are in relation to God. Our experiences of limitedness, brokenness, vulnerability and lack of wholeness are aspects of a finite being's longing for the infinite. In our society where people are valued by what they own and what they have achieved, people can be caught in a never-ending drive for more; believing that there is something just beyond their grasp that would lay their striving to rest. Most often we turn to creatures rather than to the Creator. But these earthly goods do not satisfy the hunger nor quench the thirst for more. Individuals, groups and countries set up structures and systems to establish, defend and promote the accumulation and concentration of wealth and power in the hands of a few. But acquisition is only one side. Deprivation – poverty, dishonour and powerlessness – is the other side of the coin.

The triple temptation of Jesus can be seen as a dramatic presentation of what happened throughout his ministry. But he refused wealth, honour and power. These were not the means to establish God's Kingdom. These earthly goods would not make him the Messiah. Instead, he sought solitude. He went out to pray. He turned to the Father for comfort and rest.

Poverty does not exist in isolation from wealth. The two are intricately linked. The Bible understands this well. Several terms are used in Scripture to denote the poor. But the root words point in one direction. The poor are the deprived, oppressed and exploited. If human beings turn to God rather than to earthly goods to heal their brokenness, will policies, structures and systems to eradicate poverty fall into place? Isaiah 58 is a call for true penitence. The first part exposes the sins of the people and exhorts them to the fasting that pleases God, not outward religiosity, but rather the removal of outward injustice and oppression. The second part outlines the promise of restoration that comes after genuine repentance. Material and spiritual blessings will fall on everyone.

The session on education shows the struggle and dream of a member of an ethnic minority to gain educational competence so that she can become a teacher to her own people. For her, education is not just a means to earn a living, it is a gift to be shared with others. Erna's story is also the tale of a faith-inspired organisation to serve those in greatest need. Jesus' option for the poor is re-lived among the most disadvantaged people in the Philippines. The opposite of love is not hate. It is selfishness. Erna and the Community Action for Rural Development (CARD) show that conversion is changing the focus from self to the oppressed and marginalized.

In session three Julie asks, 'What sin have I committed for which I am being punished?' She is infected with HIV/AIDS. Are we moved with compassion? Or do we believe that this is God's way of controlling population explosion? Or are these people just reaping the fruits of their immoral behaviour? Jesus lived with people who believed that infirmities were effects of sin. Is our God a God of compassion or a God of wrath? Jesus was so moved, 'down to his guts', that he healed the sick, fed the hungry and raised a son back to life. What is our response to this pandemic?

The session on trade challenges the understanding of justice based on neutrality and objectivity. The issue at the heart of trade is not misunderstanding. It is the problem of injustice and oppression. Our God is a God who hears the cry of the oppressed. Meiri and the women in her village found an alternative livelihood through their co-operative. Many other people are not as fortunate. Unjust trade rules are systematically depriving people of their livelihood. Participants are challenged to join a global movement for justice so that trade rules are weighted to benefit the poor and the planet.

These sessions focus on our role to proclaim God's reign through words and deeds. The last study reminds us that we are vessels of clay. We are weak and small, but we do not despair because God is with us. In the weakness of the cross Jesus was used by God in the ultimate act of self denial and sacrifice, which opened the way for resurrection and new life. Above all we should keep our faith and hope because the final establishment of the Kingdom is God's gift. We start with our poverty of being and finish with our weakness and fallibility. But with Paul we affirm, 'I can do all things through him who strengthens me.' (Philippians 4: 13)

Romy Tiongco and Myrna Bajo

SESSION ONE:

POVERTY

As a deer longs for flowing streams, so my soul longs for you, O God.

Psalm 42: 1

Welcome and Introduction (5 minutes)

Welcome to this first session of our Lenten study.
During the next few weeks we will be listening to some voices from "the South" – the developing countries of the world. Their stories illustrate the struggle between death and life, between oppression and justice and liberation. We are invited to look for parallels with the passion and ultimate victory of Jesus over death, and also to reflect on the relevance of these stories to us, and the challenge they present to us in our own walk with God.

Today we will explore together the theme of Poverty. At the turn of the century world governments agreed an ambitious target of halving the number of people who live in absolute poverty by 2015. Only 10 years are left to achieve this goal. Has much really changed since the 1960s?
The world's poor work harder than the rest of humanity but they have too little food, are often ill, bullied and oppressed and have little control over their lives. Development agencies seek to support them in the struggle to improve their lives. But the world's population continues to grow. There are now more people living in absolute poverty than ever before. Also, the gap between rich and poor across the globe and within individual countries is widening. Better governments, more business investments, and active participation in campaigns and advocacy are needed to achieve the millennium targets.

Most Bible translations render Matthew 5: as 'Blessed are the poor in spirit'. But the New English Bible translates it as 'How blest are those who know their need of God.' The poor have nothing and have no-one to rely on. And yet if they are spiritually rich they do not despair. God is their Rock, their Shield, their Stronghold, their Refuge – the God whom they trust.

The spiritually poor, on the other hand, are like the rich fool in Luke 12: 13-21. They do not know their need of God. They put their trust in other things, including material possessions.

Being wealthy does not necessarily mean that one is spiritually poor, but the followers of Jesus are invited to serve God. They cannot serve both God and Mammon. They must make a choice. They are challenged to live the paradox that it is in giving that they receive; in dying that they are re-born. When God becomes the treasure, one is freed from the enslavement of earthly possessions. Giving and sharing, rather than accumulation and hoarding, become the dominant behaviour pattern. Paul is a shining example:

> Yet whatever gains I had, these I have come to regard as loss because of Christ. More than that, I regard everything as loss because of the surpassing value of knowing Christ Jesus my Lord. For his sake I have suffered the loss of all things, and I regard them as rubbish, in order that I may gain Christ…
>
> Philippians 3: 7-8

Indeed, 'Has not God chosen the poor in the world to be rich in faith and to be heirs of the kingdom that he has promised to those who love him?' (James 2:5)

As Christians we are urged by Jesus to care for the poor and act with justice to combat oppression. A great challenge faces us in the contrasts we see between material wealth and poverty in the world around us. At the same time, perhaps, we can learn from those who are materially poor, but often blessed with spiritual riches.

Opening Worship (10 minutes)

You may like to sing 'As the deer pants for the water' (Mission Praise 37), or recite it as a prayer, or use this prayer, with the voice of two groups or two individuals:

All: **As a deer longs for flowing streams, so my soul longs for you, O God.**

Voice 1: My soul thirsts for God, for the living God. When shall I come and behold the face of God? My tears have been my food day and night, while people say to me continually, 'Where is your God?'

All: **As a deer longs for flowing streams, so my soul longs for you, O God.**

Voice 2: Deep calls to deep at the thunder of your cataracts; all your waves and your billows have gone over me. By day the Lord commands his steadfast love, and at night his song is with me, a prayer to the God of my life.

All: **As a deer longs for flowing streams, so my soul longs for you, O God.**

Voice 1: I say to God, my rock, 'Why have you forgotten me? Why must I walk about mournfully because the enemy oppresses me?' As with a deadly wound in my body, my adversaries taunt me, while they say to me continually 'Where is your God?'

All: **As a deer longs for flowing streams, so my soul longs for you, O God.**

Voice 2: Why are you cast down, O my soul, and why are you disquieted within me? Hope in God; for I shall again praise him, my help and my God.

All: **As a deer longs for flowing streams, so my soul longs for you, O God.**

Let us pray:

O God, you made us for yourself so we long for you. But often we turn to other creatures instead of coming to you, our Creator. Enable us to expose to you the emptiness of our inner selves. Come and fill up the void that you alone can adequately satisfy.

Amen.

Explore (20 minutes)

Group exercise: 'The Step Forward Game'

(15 minutes)

The facilitator allocates to everyone in the group a character from the list on page 62 (Facilitators' Notes). Everyone stands side by side in a straight line at one end of the room, all facing the same way.

The facilitator reads out the following questions to all the participants, one by one, asking each player to decide if, as their given character, they can answer "yes" or "no". If a player decides they can answer "yes" they take one step forward. Try not to discuss the answers too much at this stage. This continues until all the questions have been asked.

Questions for characters in the game

1. Do you know where you are going to sleep tonight?
2. After you have paid all your housing and food costs, can you afford a holiday?
3. Do you know where to get good advice on housing and legal/financial issues in your own language?
4. Do you feel confident that you will still have a home if you retire or change your job?
5. Are you able to give a fixed home address to Social Services, GP, retailers and banks?
6. Can you / your family afford to eat a balanced diet?

After all the questions have been asked, come back together as a group and discuss:

- How did you feel about your role and the things you could/could not do?
- Were there some factors which tended to benefit some characters consistently?

Reflect (10 minutes)

Robin's experience

When Robin was at college, he knew what he wanted in life. By the age of forty-five he would have a beautiful wife and two children, a house in a prosperous neighbourhood, an executive job, a healthy savings account, a Mercedes Benz, and opportunities to travel abroad. It was a long list. But he was lucky. By his mid-forties he had achieved everything he had wished for. But the quest was not over. Somehow Robin still felt empty inside. He didn't seem to be able to reach out to his wife any more, he had become like a stranger to her. The children seemed to be interested in him only for what he could buy them. Rising so quickly up the ladder at work had made him few friends. He was sick of hotel rooms, which all seemed to look the same, in whatever country they were. He knew that others were envious of him, for being so well known, having such wealth and power. But he felt a kind of bitterness. Getting what he had longed for had not quenched his hunger and thirst for them. Instead, the desire for more became more intense and compelling.

Silent Reflection:

Unless the participants prefer to share their thoughts, this time can be devoted to silent reflection.

Encourage participants to close their eyes, breathe deeply and gently and quietly pray 'Come, Lord Jesus. Come.' The petition can be made repeatedly.

Reading and Listening (5 minutes)

Voice from the South

An Economy Based on Solidarity.

Honduras has been plagued by so-called natural disasters over the past few years. Hurricane Mitch caused mass destruction in 1998, destroying agricultural produce and stocks. This was followed by drought in 1999, floods in 2000, and then drought followed by floods in 2001. Although often called 'natural' disasters, they have unnatural consequences and unnatural root causes. Global warming, caused by carbon emissions mostly coming from the rich countries of the 'North', inflicts severe suffering on the poor countries of the 'South'. With limited resources and a poor infrastructure, Honduras really struggled to cope with these disasters.

COMAL is an acronym of the Spanish name for Alternative Community Marketing Network in Honduras. When Mitch struck the country, COMAL provided emergency relief and long-term rehabilitation and reconstruction programmes. Eventually it moved back to long-term development work. COMAL builds the relationship between producers and consumers on fair price, high quality products and the direct involvement of communities. As the Executive Director says,

> 'By developing a community-based solidarity, we work to assure food security and jobs at local level, but also the volume of trade to operate at national level. COMAL believes that together we can construct an economic alternative for people if we respect the rights of people and practise justice.'

COMAL helps communities by guaranteeing a regular and a fair price for their produce. It also organises the marketing and distribution of these essential products, so ensuring that none of its members go hungry.

In 2000 COMAL had a profit of £700,000 and re-invested most of the money back into its communities. It puts people before profit and firmly believes that this model can be replicated all over the country. Bautistina manages one of COMAL's distribution and consumers co-operative stores.

When she was asked why the shop operated the way it did, she replied:

'Jesus came to serve us, so we want to follow His example and serve others.'

God's Word

The Rich Young Man (Mark 10:17-22)

As he was setting out on a journey, a man ran up and knelt before him, and asked him, 'Good Teacher, what must I do to inherit eternal life?' Jesus said to him, 'Why do you call me good? No one is good but God alone. You know the commandments: "You shall not murder; You shall not commit adultery; You shall not steal; You shall not bear false witness; You shall not defraud; Honour your father and mother."' He said to him, 'Teacher, I have kept all these since my youth.'

Jesus, looking at him, loved him and said, 'You lack one thing; go, sell what you own, and give the money to the poor, and you will have treasure in heaven; then come, follow me.' When he heard this, he was shocked and went away grieving, for he had many possessions.

Discussion (30 minutes)

The 'hard sayings' of Jesus is the term used to describe the warnings he issued about the dangers of material possessions. Instead of owning them, they possess us. They become our treasure. And where our treasure is, there our hearts will be also (Matthew 6: 21). We are unable to love God. We become incapable of loving our neighbour. We become the slaves of Mammon. No wonder Jesus warned, 'How hard it is for those who have wealth to enter the kingdom of God!' (Luke 18: 24) It is refreshing how Aloysius Pieris, S.J., a Sri Lankan theologian, rephrases Jesus' invitation to the rich young man. The invitation is not to give up his wealth – full stop. It is to sell his possessions and to give the money to the poor. The moral advice is 'Strive to be poor so that no-one will be poor'. Love of God and love of neighbour enable a person to choose voluntary poverty so that no one will be trapped in forced poverty. In the Bible the perspective that sees poverty as a result of injustice, oppression and exploitation is very dominant.

a. How relevant is Jesus' invitation to the rich young man to people like Robin?

b. How is the invitation which Jesus makes to the young man lived out by the COMAL co-operative?

c. If COMAL's success in tackling poverty comes out of an approach based on fairness, justice and compassion, are we able, as individuals and churches, to use a similar approach to tackle poverty?

d. How would we react if Jesus invited us to do the same thing? Why? Can his invitation to us refer to things other than money?

Moving Forward (5 minutes)

Read the following poem, composed by Javier Torres of Nicaragua in 1992.

If the hunger of others is not my own,
If the anguish of my neighbour in all its forms touches me not,
If the nakedness of my brother or sister does not torment me,
then I have no reason to go to church and live.
Life is this: to love one's neighbour as oneself;
this is the commandment of God.
Love means deeds, not good wishes.
For this reason I commit myself to working
for the necessities of my brothers and sisters.

During the next week consider:

- What practical actions or decisions can we take to so that those who have less may have more, in order to be more?

Closing Worship (10 minutes)

Call to worship: 'The Lord gave, and the Lord has taken away; blessed be the name of the Lord.'

Solo: We live in a world, which progressively blurs the distinction between necessity, comfort and luxury so that we are unable to tell the difference.

All: **My soul is restless and it shall remain restless until it rests in you, O God.**

Solo: Money offers everything – material possessions, influence, status, power, and happiness. It is God's rival.

All: **My soul is restless and it shall remain restless until it rests in you, O God.**

Solo: We are constantly bombarded by the idea that who we are is measured by what we have.

All: **My soul is restless and it shall remain restless until it rests in you, O God.**

Let us pray:

**Grant us courage to learn poverty, that we may discover your riches;
to become foolish, so that we may speak with your wisdom;
to celebrate weakness, resting in your strength;
to rejoice in being nothing, because Christ has become all things.
Amen.**

Suggested songs for opening/closing worship

As the deer pants for the water	MP 37
The Lord's my Shepherd	CG127, CH3 387
Brother, Sister, let me serve you	CG 16
O God of our divided world	CH3 506
(tune, Warrington, CH3 413)	

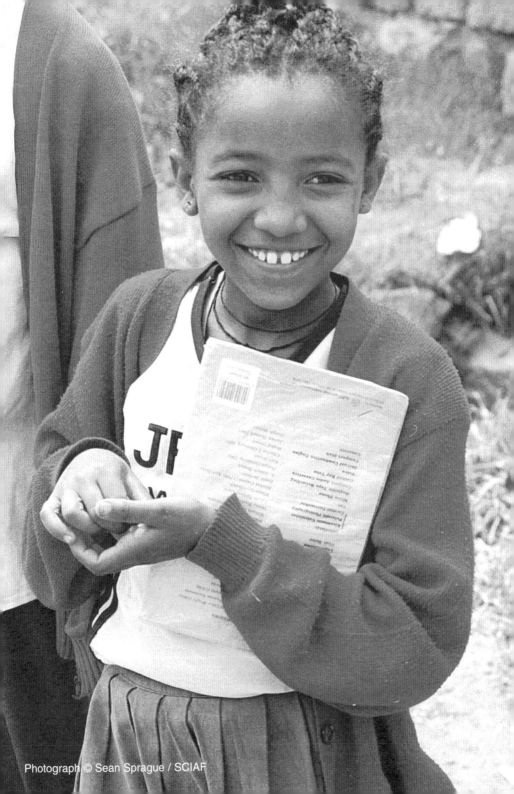

SESSION TWO:

EDUCATION

Then you will understand righteousness and justice and equity,
every good path;
for wisdom will come into your heart, and knowledge
will be pleasant to your soul;
prudence will watch over you; and understanding
will guard you.

Proverbs 3: 9-11

Looking Back (5 minutes)

Let's recall what we did at the first study session on Poverty. We didn't
focus on the poor 'out there' nor on the political and economic structural
causes of poverty. It is outmoded by at least 50 years, but I still remember
a catechism question and answer on why God created human beings. 'God
created us to know, love and serve Him and to be happy with Him forever.'

Jesus could have summoned legions of angels to come to his assistance in
Gethsemane. He didn't. Three times he went out to pray. And he begged,
'Father, if you are willing, remove this cup from me; yet not my will but
yours be done.' The Father is his God. The Father is his Happiness. Who is
our God?

Introduction and Opening Worship (10 minutes)

Our topic for today's study session is Education. One of the global targets
of the United Nations is that every child should have a primary education
by 2015, but our focus here is on a wider concern with education.

According to Anne Hope and Sally Timmel, authors of a handbook on
Training for Transformation, "Development and education are first of all
about liberating people from all that holds them back from a full human life.
Ultimately development and education are about transforming society.
Because the bonds of poverty and oppression make the lives of vast
numbers of people increasingly inhuman, it is amongst the poor and

oppressed that development programmes and education must start."

We belong to a society where acquisition of education is relatively easy. But in many other countries people do not have the same access to education. Let us therefore reflect on and explore its value as a right, a privilege and a gift that should be used to serve God and the interests of our disadvantaged brothers and sisters.

Jesus came to serve and not to be served. And this is what he wished us to do for each other when he set the example of washing the disciples' feet. In Paul's exhortation to the Corinthians about their almsgiving, he puts before them Jesus' example of self-emptying love. 'For you know the generous act of our Lord Jesus Christ, that though he was rich, yet for your sakes he became poor, so that by his poverty you might become rich.' (2 Corinthians 8: 9)

Let us have a moment's silence to listen to God's call.

Prayer

Solo: God of peace, in the waiting, which seems endless,
        for your promise of justice to be fulfilled
        for the poor, the persecuted and the oppressed:

All: School us in patience, fortitude and zeal.

Solo: As we wait with you in obscurity,
        for your truth to be revealed:

All: Prompt us to hear you and obey your teachings.

Solo: In these days when your teaching is flouted,
        your instruction ignored, your commandments broken, and
        your law cast into the mire of our indifference:

All: Grant us to revere your purposes and celebrate your acts.

Solo: And in the fullness of time, when all your work is complete,
        your plans brought to fruition, and the fragments of your dream
        brought into one:

All: Gather us with the broken pieces of your making, into the glorious crown of your new creation.

Let us pray:

Solo: Lord we know that as you grew you increased in wisdom, in years and in divine and human favour. Teach us to value the quiet time for prayer, study and preparation and bless our activities with your presence.

All: Amen.

Reading and Listening

God's Word (5 minutes)

Becoming wise (Proverbs 2: 1-11)

My child, if you accept my words and treasure up my commandments within you,
making your ear attentive to wisdom and inclining your heart to understanding;
if you indeed cry out for insight, and raise your voice for understanding;
if you seek it like silver, and search for it as for hidden treasures -
then you will understand the fear of the Lord and find the knowledge of God.
For the Lord gives wisdom; from his mouth come knowledge and understanding;
he stores up sound wisdom for the upright; he is a shield to those who walk blamelessly,
guarding the paths of justice and preserving the way of his faithful ones.
Then you will understand righteousness and justice and equity, every good path;
for wisdom will come into your heart, and knowledge will be pleasant to your soul;
prudence will watch over you; and understanding will guard you.

Wisdom (Proverbs 9: 8-11)

"Wisdom" says:
A scoffer who is rebuked will only hate you;
the wise, when rebuked, will love you.
Give instruction to the wise, and they will become wiser still;
Teach the righteous and they will gain in learning.
The fear of the Lord is the beginning of wisdom, and the knowledge of the Holy One is insight.
For by me your days will be multiplied, and years will be added to your life.

Explore (20 minutes)

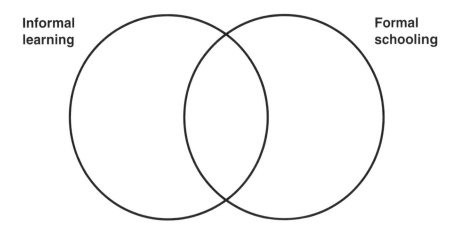

Informal learning

Formal schooling

Look at the reading from Proverbs.

There are so many things we can learn, such as wisdom, knowledge, to treasure God's commandments etc.

How many of these can come through formal education or 'schooling', how many through wider, more informal learning, and how many by both these routes? Discuss this in twos or threes and write the words onto the interlocking circles.

Still in twos or threes, discuss:
a. Has your education benefited you? How?
b. How does our education system benefit society as a whole?
c. Would we be able to learn so much informally, if we did not have a tradition of good schooling influencing the prevailing culture?

Reading and Listening (5 minutes)

Voice from the South

Erna's Story

Mindanao, in the Philippines, is home to numerous tribes and migrant settlers, but the population can be classified into three main groups: the Christian majority (over 15 million), the Muslims (almost 5 million) and the Lumads (about 2 million). They have been living together on the island for over a century, but the Christians enjoy better access to services, control over resources and of governance.

The Lumads are the indigenous peoples who have held on to the beliefs and ways of life of their forebears. They have been slowly but effectively dispossessed of their rights to land. They are perceived to be difficult to deal with because they lack education and are considered primitive and backward. There are very few efforts to relate to them on their own terms. Instead the formal education system sees to it that they learn how to speak, read and write in a language that is not their own. They are thus forced to adapt to the migrants' way of life. The only form of representation that they have is through their tribal councils, but these do not have a voice in government.

Lumad culture has been conveniently commercialised for the sake of tourism and 'cultural preservation'. They are kept as living museum pieces and unable to integrate with the general population. Community Action for Rural Development (CARD) works with the Lumads. Although it is a faith-based organisation, it is not institutionally linked with a Christian Church. Through CARD's ministry, changes are emerging. Erna's story embodies struggle and hope.

'My father did not appreciate the value of education. He preferred that the children all helped in farm work. I cried when my classmates went on to finish primary education. I envied the few who proceeded to go to high school. As for me, I was kept in the farm to take care of my mother who was sick with tuberculosis.'

When the Regional Department of Health conducted training in microscopy, CARD recommended Erna, one of its Community Health Workers, to take the course. She was proud to complete it successfully. Although she only finished Grade 2, she topped the class of 13 trainees. Two were graduates in Medical Technology and the others had finished primary or high school.

Erna is now 20 years old and has a two-year old daughter. Her husband understands and supports her dream and commitment. As a Community Medical Technologist under the Rural Health Unit she is responsible for conducting blood, sputum and stool examinations. She also provides medicine for specific types of malaria and refers those found positive for TB or those who need treatment for specific types of intestinal parasites to the Rural Health Unit.

Erna's dream is to acquire a higher level of formal education. She realises that she has the intellectual capacity to do so. She is interested in the Non-Formal Education programme run by the Department of Education. This programme provides a modular type of education with minimum structured instruction. After this she plans to pursue formal schooling and hopes to become a teacher. Her tribe has never had a dedicated teacher and the children are unable to receive good quality education.

'I know that it will be difficult to attend classes in the town centre even for only 5 days a month for 20 months. The trip back and forth to my mountain village is formidable. But I will take up the challenge. The important thing is that I will qualify for college. God-willing, I will be a teacher of my tribe ... SOMEDAY.'

Discussion (35 minutes)

Jesus' 'hidden life' is truly hidden. The concluding sentence of the episode of him being separated from his parents in the Temple simply states, 'And Jesus increased in wisdom and in years, and in divine and human favour.' (Luke 2:2) Then Luke immediately writes about John the Baptist. But during those silent years, he learned something – a lot! The crowds were astounded at this teaching. He taught with authority (Matthew 7:28). He invited those who were tired and weary because his yoke was easy and his burden light. But he was critical of the religious leaders who did exactly the opposite by using their learning and scholarship to impose prescriptive external rituals and laws which were difficult to follow, 'heavy burdens, hard to bear' (Matthew 23:4). It is inspiring to hear what Erna plans to do with her life and her ambition to become a teacher.

We need education to get a job. No skills, no job – this is the simple equation that we frequently hear. Knowledge and skills are definitely very important, but is education simply a **means** to get a job? What about attitudes? What about values? Why do we want education?

In Scripture wisdom is knowledge dedicated to the purposes of God. It involves fear of the Lord, knowledge of God, justice, righteousness and equity.

a. How does our education system stand alongside these values?

b. How does the writer of Proverbs describe the value of 'education'? What other benefits go hand in hand with the 'wisdom the Lord gives'?

c. Solomon found great favour with God when, in humility, he asked for wisdom, (1 Kings 3:7-14) and his wisdom and knowledge brought him wealth, power and status. It was not enough, however, to assure his righteousness when he failed to put God first. Can the pursuit of education bring dangers, or will increasing knowledge always bring good?

d. How important is Erna's dream to the future of her people? How does this compare with the experiences of past or present missionaries sent by our churches?

e. To the wise of the world, Jesus was a fool. His teachings and his living them out brought him death on the cross. Has Christian education lost its sting?

Moving Forward

In the coming week:

* Undertake some research into exactly what the Millennium Goals on education are. (One useful website: www.un.org/millenniumgoals)

* Find out if your church is involved with overseas mission programmes concerned with education. What are their problems? Is there any way that you can be of help?

Closing Worship (10 minutes)

The participants divide into two groups and recite the first part of this prayer antiphonally. Alternatively it can be read by two individuals.
The verses are from Proverbs 3: 5-8; 13-14; 27-28.

**Trust in the Lord with all your heart,
and do not rely on your own insight.**

In all your ways acknowledge him,
and he will make straight your paths.

**Do not be wise in your own eyes;
fear the Lord, and turn away from evil.**

It will be healing for your flesh
and refreshment for your body.

**Happy are those who find wisdom,
and those who get understanding,**

for her income is better than silver,
and her revenue better than gold.

Do not withhold good from those to whom it is due, when it is in your power to do it.

Do not say to your neighbour, 'Go and come again; tomorrow I will give it' – when you have it with you.

Let us pray:

All:

God, you are all-knowing.
You know our thoughts, our aspirations, and our hopes.
And you want us to grow in knowledge, in understanding, in wisdom.
We thank you Lord for the opportunities you have given us to achieve your plans for us.

But many of your poor children don't have as many opportunities in life as we and our children have.

Many in poor countries long for education but have no access to it, either because of dire poverty, or because the nearest schools are many miles walk away.

Inspire changes in individuals and education policies so that in the new structures your beloved poor will enjoy opportunities to grow in knowledge, in understanding and in wisdom.

Amen.

Suggested songs for opening/closing worship

Amazing grace	CG 6, MP 31
Will you come and follow me	CG 148
I, the Lord of sea and sky	CG 50
Thou art the way	CH3 121, MP 695

LETSFIGHT

AIDS

orld

Reme

is all

tude

SESSION THREE:

HEALTH

His disciples asked him, 'Rabbi, who sinned, this man or his parents, that he was born blind?' Jesus answered, 'Neither this man nor his parents sinned; he was born blind so that God's works might be revealed in him.'

John 9: 2-3

Looking Back (5 minutes)

Lack of education is both a cause and an effect of poverty. Erna has sprung the trap. But it is most refreshing that her ambition to move on is tied up with her desire to go back to her community. Lack of education is one reason why her people are being excluded and marginalized. She wants to rejoin them so that together they can move forward.

Jesus came so that we may 'have life and have it to the full' (John 10:10). He proclaimed that the Kingdom of God is here. Erna is making her contribution to make 'a pocket' of the Kingdom a reality in her people's lives.

Introduction

Today we will look at another effect that also worsens the experience of living in poverty. It started as a health problem but it is now considered a major development issue. In a number of countries in the South, the economically productive generation is dying. The surviving families are composed of young children and elderly grandparents. Parents have become the missing generation.

The voices from the South portray suffering and pain, but not despair. God's liberating love is working in people as they plant the seeds of hope and strive towards fuller lives. People who live in desperate situations can be the most eloquent preachers of hope. Their deeds abound in courage, power and inspiration.

Opening Worship (10 minutes)

Solo: Lord, God, you have shown us by your example your compassion for people with unattractive conditions - the blind, the lame, the crippled, the lepers and the prostitutes.
In our times, Lord, you are giving us other people with similar conditions - the alcoholics and drug addicts, and those affected by HIV/AIDS.

Touch their hearts, O God, and make them turn towards you, that they may feel their value, that they are accepted and loved.

All: **Let them not lose hope in your healing grace. Let them put their confidence in your compassion and in your ways of re-creation.**

Solo: Loving God, we know that you do not wish pain on anyone, however blameworthy. In your mercy it is never too late for us to turn to you, repenting of our sins of commission and omission, and asking for forgiveness. Touch our hearts, O God, that we may reach out to them through our prayers and offerings.

All: **Let us not fall into believing that we are holier than them, for we all are your children, and we all need your continuing salvation.**

Solo: Forgive us merciful God, for the stigma laid on them by our society, our church, ourselves. So for them, for ourselves, and for the human family of which we are part, we ask you:

All: **Let our hearts and minds be cleansed and purified by the fire of your love, O Lord our God.**

Amen

Explore (20 minutes)

Facing the Pandemic

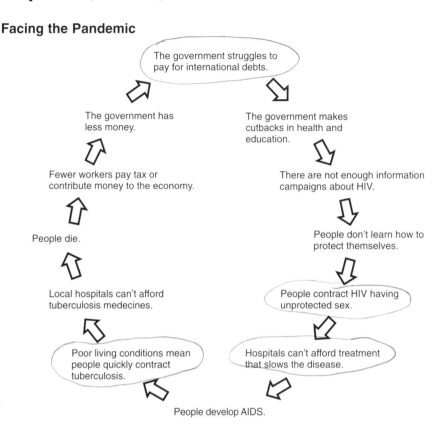

From the cycle above, discuss in twos or threes:

• What did these people die of – AIDS, immorality, ignorance, poverty?

• Which bits in the cycle need to be changed to stop the vicious circle?

• Look at the statements in the following table. Decide as a group whether you agree or disagree with them. Does it make any difference whether they refer to people in the 'North' (so-called developed countries) or the 'South' (developing countries)? If so, why?

	North		South	
	Agree	Disagree	Agree	Disagree
1. People living with HIV/AIDS are usually responsible in some way for their condition				
2. Fewer people would be infected with HIV if there was better education about the virus				
3. Help should be offered to anyone living with HIV/AIDS without judgement				
4. The most effective treatments should be available to all HIV positive individuals				
5. Christians have a particular responsibility to show compassion to those living with HIV/AIDS				

Reading and Listening

God's Word (5 minutes)

Jesus Heals a Leper (Mark 1: 40-44)

A leper came to him begging him, and kneeling he said to him, 'If you choose, you can make me clean.' Moved with pity, Jesus stretched out his hand and touched him, and said to him, 'I do choose. Be made clean!' Immediately the leprosy left him, and he was made clean. After sternly warning him he sent him away at once, saying to him, 'See that you say nothing to anyone; but go, show yourself to the priest, and offer for your cleansing what Moses commanded, as a testimony to them.'

Jesus Heals a Man Born Blind (John 9: 2-9)

His disciples asked him, 'Rabbi, who sinned, this man or his parents, that he was born blind?' Jesus answered, 'Neither this man nor his parents sinned; he was born blind so that God's works might be revealed in him. We must work the works of him who sent me while it is day; night is coming when no one can work. As long as I am in the world, I am the light of the world.' When he had said this, he spat on the ground and made mud with the saliva and spread the mud on the man's eyes, saying to him, 'Go, wash in the pool of Siloam' (which means Sent). Then he went and washed and came back able to see. The neighbours and those who had seen him before as a beggar began to ask, 'Is this not the man who used to sit and beg?' Some were saying, 'It is he.' Others were saying, 'No, but it is someone like him.' He kept saying, 'I am the man.'

Voice from the South

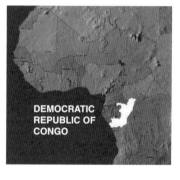

Julie's Story

Continuing conflict in the Democratic Republic of Congo has had a crippling effect on the country's economy, with schools, hospitals and communications all in a very poor condition. HIV/AIDS is a serious problem, compounded by the acute poverty in the country and minimal government spending on health. The national percentage of the population, which is HIV-positive, is between 5 and 10 per cent, but in areas of conflict it is very much higher.

Most countries in the South do not have adequate (state) welfare services. HIV/AIDS is no longer just a health issue but has become a development problem. This pandemic in sub-Saharan Africa has already reached crisis proportions. A total of 17 million people have already died there. In Botswana one in three people are expected to die in the next few years. In Zimbabwe life expectancy which in 1993 was 61, has fallen to 39 and continues to fall. Across the continent 12.1 million children have lost one or both parents to HIV/AIDS and many of them are infected themselves. As the productive generations die, the survivors are old grandparents and young children.

Julie is from Kinshasa, Democratic Republic of Congo. She prefers to tell her own story:

> 'I was proud of my height and my beauty. Two men wanted to marry me, one who was a mechanic and the other, a man who had a car. I accepted the proposal from the man who owned a car. Without having an HIV test, we got married. I became pregnant and we had a little girl. She became ill and died shortly after. I, too, became ill and went to see a doctor who confirmed I was HIV positive. I was very shocked and did a lot of thinking and praying.
>
> I decided to get a divorce and went to live with my parents. They died and life became very difficult for me and my younger brothers and sisters. No one could help us. We lost our house and had to sleep outside. My friends deserted me. I felt totally alone and I had a skin infection all over my body. I asked myself, "What have I done to merit this kind of life? What sin have I committed for which I am being punished?"
>
> Then I heard about the Fondation Femme Plus (FFP). They really helped me with food and medical care. Despite my illness I do have hope. I joined FFP's photography project. It has helped me. It has made me more open about myself and I am proud that my photos will be shown abroad.'

Discussion (30 minutes)

It has been said that Jesus' compassion was not only an emotional reaction but also an indictment of the numbness and self-righteousness of the dominant culture towards the marginalized, the harassed and helpless.

a. During Jesus' time people with leprosy were ostracised and rejected. They were considered unclean. It was assumed that their sickness was punishment for their sins. How is this attitude reflected in our own times with regard to HIV/AIDS?

b. How would you respond to Julie's question: 'What sin have I committed for which I am being punished?'

c.   How does the healing of the leper in chapter 3 of Mark and the man born blind in chapter 9 of John:

1. challenge our own attitudes to sickness, health, healing and wholeness?
2. shed light on Julie's experience?

d.   How can Jesus' passion and death be a source of strength for those suffering because of HIV/AIDS?

Moving Forward (5 minutes)

Facts and Figures: Spread of HIV/AIDS across the regions

North America	- 980,000
Western Europe	- 570,000
Eastern Europe and Central Asia	- 1.2 million
East Asia and Pacific	- 1.2 million
South and South East Asia	- 6.0 million
North Africa and Middle East	- 550,000
Latin America	- 1.5 million
Australia and New Zealand	- 15,000
Sub-Saharan Africa	- 29.4 million

The compassion of Jesus should challenge any moral resistance we have to feel sympathy with people living with HIV/AIDS. But we need more than a change in attitude. What about knowledge and skills?

During the week ahead:

•   Find out about HIV/AIDS in your area.

•   Consider: are there ways in which you can help?

Closing Worship (10 minutes)

Let us pray:

All: **Lord, help us to accept the challenge of HIV/AIDS:**
to protect the healthy, calm the fearful;
to offer courage to those in pain;
to embrace the dying;
to console the bereaved;
to support all those who attempt to care for the sick and dying.

Voice 1: Jeanne, a married woman from Burundi, has publicly acknowledged that she has AIDS and has founded a national association for people who are HIV-positive. She says that people come to her when they want to pray but think they are too wicked for God to hear.

'But suffering is the face of God. It is for this moment, when you turn to him in need and fear, that God has been waiting and longing,' Jeanne replies.

Voice 2: We give you thanks, O God, that you gave us your Son Jesus Christ, who for our sake became poor. We thank you that through his grace, though we are broken we are made whole; though we have fallen we are lifted up, we are forgiven, loved and freed. And we trust that as you have exalted him, so you will also raise us up, from sorrow to joy, from doubt to certainty, from pain to peace, and from death to eternal life.

Voice 1: Gaia from South Africa is HIV-positive. She runs her own cleaning company and belongs to a warm and welcoming church community. But she is afraid that if people in her church found out they would reject her.
Gaia says: 'God knows. God doesn't reject.'

Voice 2: Lord, may we go where the darkness is and stand together there, alongside people with HIV/AIDS and those whose lives are affected by it; may we face with you the terrible uncertainty of tomorrow: of what will happen, what might happen, what could happen, to children and families, to work and relationships, to our world. Lord, hear this and all our prayers in the name of him who came to feed the hungry and heal the sick, your Son our Saviour, Jesus Christ. Amen.

Final Prayer:

All: **Loving God,**
You show yourself in those who are vulnerable,
and make your home with the poor and weak of this
world.
Warm our hearts with the fire of your spirit,
and help us to accept the challenges of AIDS.

May we, your people, using all our energy and
imagination,
and trusting in your steadfast love,
be united with one another in conquering disease
and fear.
We make this prayer in the name of one who has
borne all our wounds,
and whose Spirit strengthens and guides us,
now and for ever.

Amen.

Suggested songs for opening/closing worship

Eat this bread, drink this cup   CG 31
Lord we come to ask your healing   CG 78
May the mind of Christ my Saviour   CH3 432 MP 463
I need thee   CH3 688 MP 288

check newspaper — *Fairtrade* *bright details*
WDM / trade justice each etc
Bits water campaign
wear Fairtrade clothes.
Big catalogues
EPAs
SATs

SESSION FOUR:

TRADE

Ah, you who make iniquitous decrees, who write oppressive statutes, to turn
aside the needy from justice and to rob the poor of my people of their right,
that widows may be your spoil, and that you may make the orphans your prey!
What will you do on the day of punishment, in the calamity that will come
from far away?

IMF

Isaiah 10:1-3

Looking Back and Introduction (5 minutes)

It would be good to have a few moments of silence to pray for our brothers
and sisters who passed away during the past week due to HIV/AIDS. In
Soweto, South Africa alone, there are a hundred funerals a day, mainly of
young or middle aged adults.

During this session we hope to gain a deeper appreciation of the unique
contribution that our faith tradition brings to the understanding of justice. It
is a voice and a witness that needs to be heard, and needs to inform
policies and laws, so that everyone and the planet can benefit from trade. A
change in perspective demands repentance. We cannot just stand and
watch – a sin of omission – a few hoarding the benefits of international
trade, while the majority are denied their fair share. Surely we are called to
conversion from apathy and resignation to pro-active involvement in the
campaign for justice in the international laws governing trade. Jesus
affirmed the prophetic demands for justice in his 'mission statement'. (Luke
4: 18-21)

we are all involved here. we are all consumers

Opening Worship (10 minutes)

check

Read the following prayer, using the voices of two groups or two individuals:

Solo: (1) God of the just weight and the fair measure,
Let me remember the hands
that harvested my food, my drink,
Not only in my prayers but in the market place.
Let me not seek a bargain that leaves others hungry.

41

(2) Group 1: A false balance is an abomination to the Lord, but an accurate weight is his delight. (Proverbs 11.1)

(3) Group 2: Let justice roll down like waters, and righteousness like an ever-flowing stream. (Amos 5.24)

Group 1: What does the Lord require of you but to do justice, and to love kindness, and to walk humbly with your God? (Micah 6:8)

Group 2: To do righteousness and justice is more acceptable to the Lord than sacrifice. (Proverbs 21.3)

Solo: Lord you have given us a world full of rich resources, enough for all, yet injustice remains, the poor are still with us. Lord, give us ears and eyes open to injustices, hearts committed to challenging oppression, minds focused on designing alternatives, and hands joined in solidarity to make change a reality.

All: **Amen.**

Explore (25 minutes)

'It's not fair trade' Quiz

The group splits into two – a 'poor' group and a 'wealthy West' group. The 'poor' group is given several coffee beans, the 'wealthy' group three times as many. Do the following quiz in the two groups with the Facilitator as quiz master (the correct answers can be found on page 63 in the Facilitators' Notes). You could perhaps have leaflets about fair trade available, to which only the 'wealthy' group has access.

After completing the quiz, for each correct answer the 'wealthy' group gets four beans, the 'poor' group gets one.

Then come back as a group to discuss your answers and think about the follow-up questions.

Quiz

1. The eight richest and most powerful countries (G8) of the world promised a £100 billion debt cancellation. By comparison, how much money does the UN estimate the poor countries are losing every year as a result of unjust trading rules?
    a. $ 600 billion
    b. $ 500 billion
    c. $ 700 billion

2. Trade rules are negotiated at the World Trade Organisation. Half of the world's poorest countries cannot afford to have any representatives. Japan, by contrast, has
    a. 20
    b. 12
    c. 25

3. Over the past 20 years, poor countries have been forced to slash the financial help that they used to give to their farmers. By contrast, rich countries support their farmers with annual subsidies worth
    a. $ 262 billion
    b. $ 362 billion
    c. $ 500 billion

4. There are no rules to regulate global corporations, despite their size and power. General Motors, for example, is as rich as how many of the world's poorest countries put together?
    a. 37
    b. 25
    c. 20

5. The retail price of chocolate has increased by over 60% in the last 10 years. By what percentage has the price for cocoa beans increased?
    a. increased by 25%
    b. decreased by 25%
    c. decreased by 50%

6. Which supermarket's own brand chocolate is entirely Fairtrade?
    a. Co-op
    b. Safeway
    c. Tesco

43

7. Poor countries are prevented from providing subsidies to their farmers because:
    a. their financial reserves are very low
    b. their products are more cheaply produced in other countries
    c. it is a condition attached to the giving of loans by International Financial Institutions

8. "Trade opportunity cost" is possible income lost as a result of:
    a. inferior quality of the products
    b. tariff barriers imposed especially on finished products
    c. lack of raw materials for industrial processing

9. According to the figures of a sustainable development watchdog, Redefining Progress, the lifestyle of Britain is dependent on resources (productive land and water) from outside the country. Approximately what percentage of the resources actually come from Britain?
    a. 70%
    b. 30%
    c. 50%

10. In 1998 the United States filed a case against the European Union for unfair trade practice and won. What was the product at issue?
    a. whisky
    b. sugar
    c. bananas

Follow-up to Quiz

- What did it feel like to be part of
  (a) the 'wealthy' group? (b) the 'poor' group?

Let's think about what we wear, the home appliances we use and all the other products that help us in our everyday lives. According to an environmental watchdog, about 70% of the resources needed to support our lifestyle come from outside Britain. Trade is an example of the way our lives are inter-connected with those of other peoples and lands.

- Discuss: How can we show our concern for the way workers are treated and what is happening to the environment?

+ ethical tourism

44

Reading and Listening (5 minutes)

God's Word :

④

God's laws (Luke 19: 8-9)

Zacchaeus stood there and said to the Lord, 'Look, half of my possessions, Lord, I will give to the poor; and if I have defrauded anyone of anything, I will pay back four times as much.' Then Jesus said to him, 'Today salvation has come to this house, because he too is a son of Abraham.'

⑤

(Deuteronomy 24: 14-18)

You shall not withhold the wages of poor and needy labourers, whether other Israelites or aliens who reside in your land in one of your towns. You shall pay them their wages daily before sunset, because they are poor and their livelihood depends on them; otherwise they might cry to the Lord against you, and you would incur guilt …You shall not deprive a resident alien or an orphan of justice; you shall not take a widow's garment in pledge. Remember that you were a slave in Egypt and the Lord your God redeemed you from there; therefore I command you to do this.

⑥

(Matthew 20: 8-14)

When evening came, the owner of the vineyard said to his manager, 'Call the labourers and give them their pay, beginning with the last and then going to the first.' When those hired about five o'clock came, each of them received the usual daily wage. Now when the first came, they thought they would receive more; but each of them also received the usual daily wage. And when they received it, they grumbled against the landowner, saying, 'These last worked only one hour, and you have made them equal to us who have borne the burden of the day and the scorching heat.' But he replied to one of them, 'Friend, I am doing you no wrong; did you not agree with me for the usual daily wage? Take what belongs to you and go; I choose to give to this last the same as I give to you.'

Also - Isaiah + Amos

Voice from the South

Meiri's Story ①

GHANA

This story is from Ghana. Meiri Seidu is the Chair of the Village Association in Guli and a board member of the Kaleo Baptist Women's Development Project (KBWDP). She is also a rice farmer who has enjoyed many successful harvests. She even once received the 'Rice Farmer of the Year' award. But all that is over. Rice farming, as a livelihood, is dying. The soil in Guli is very degraded. A farmer needs to apply fertilisers to gather a worthwhile harvest. One year a bag of fertiliser cost 20,000 cedis. The following year it went up to 80,000. The cost of production went sharply up, but the price of the rice plunged down. Rice farming became economically unviable. The price of rice dropped because the market was flooded with cheap imported rice from the US and Asia. And while Ghana is prevented by the International Financial Institutions from providing subsidies to its rice farmers, American farmers receive financial assistance from the US government.

But Guli is far from dead. It is vibrant. Though most of the houses are made of mud, new ones are being erected with concrete walls and corrugated iron roofs. The village is productive. The women are busy pounding shea nuts under the shade of many trees.

The women gather the nuts from the wild to produce shea nut butter. The processing of the nuts involves frying, pounding and cooking. The whole process takes about two days. The oil is used for cooking and for making soap and body cream. A person can collect two buckets of butter per week and each bucket sells for between 80,000 and 100,000 cedis at the local market. In the market town of Kumasi, a bucket of butter can sell for as much as 200,000 cedis.

Like the other women, Meiri still plants rice to provide food for her family. But she relies on the production of shea nut butter for cash income. Bit by bit, Meiri is getting a brick house built. She hopes that this project will be completed in one year.

46

Guli has won a new lease of life. But is getting involved in development work an appropriate undertaking for a preacher? Pastor John Bangonluri, the founder of KBWDP, reflects:

> 'My colleagues would have liked me to concentrate on evangelising as I'm good at this. But I don't see it as a different mission. Christ explained what missionary work is to us: helping the poor and feeding the hungry.'

Discussion (30 minutes)

Background:

- The International Monetary Fund, World Bank and World Trade Organisation prohibit poor, debt-ridden countries of the South from providing subsidy to their farmers as a condition for obtaining additional loans.
- The US and Europe spend $362 billion annually in subsidies to their farmers.
- The UN estimates that poor countries lose $700 billion of possible export income because of tariff barriers imposed by the rich countries. The tariff on an unprocessed product is low but goes up if the product is semi-processed and is even higher for finished products. ②

+ can't put tariffs on imports

These are three examples of why the Trade Justice Movement is claiming that the present trade rules are biased against the poor.

- The books of Leviticus and Deuteronomy command Israelites how to behave towards each other and towards others. God explicitly demands that His Chosen People should behave towards the weak and vulnerable in the way He treated and listened to them. This is affirmed by the parable of the labourers in the vineyard.
- Restitution is another mark of Biblical justice. Jesus praises Zacchaeus' commitment to refund four-fold all those he defrauded.

Discuss: *Jubilee - opi - keep the life gi*

    a. At the Old Bailey there is statue of a blindfolded woman holding a pair of scales. What does this say about society's understanding or definition of justice?

    b. How does the definition in a) compare with the concept of justice we can deduce from the Scripture readings?

c. How would you argue for the provision of subsidies to small rice and corn farmers, like Meiri, in low-income countries?

d. Jesus said, 'No one has greater love than this, to lay down one's life for one's friends' (John 15:13). Yet we were beneficiaries of his self-emptying love while we were still God's enemies. 'For if while we were enemies, we were reconciled to God through the death of his Son, much more surely, having been reconciled, will we be saved by his life' (Romans 5:10). How does the generosity of the owner of the vineyard compare with the rules promulgated by the richest countries of the world through the World Trade Organisation?

Moving Forward

2005 is a big year for the Trade Justice campaign. The UK Government is launching the Africa Commission report six months before the UN reviews progress towards the achievement of the Millennium Development Goals. The UK Government is taking over the Presidency of the European Union and will chair the G8. The year provides an opportunity for our government to lead in changing the trade rules so they are weighted to benefit the poor and the planet. But the political will to move against the interests of the rich and powerful can only happen if there is sufficient pressure from the general public. The first Global People's Week of Action will be held on 10-16 April.

Over the coming weeks:
*   Keep watch and be involved in campaign actions
*   Research your local outlets/ suppliers of fairly traded products

Closing Worship (10 minutes)

Call to worship: But let justice roll down like waters, and righteousness like an ever-flowing stream.

(Amos 5. 21)

Solo: Will you make time in your lives to hear the voice of God in prayer, reflected in the cry of those who suffer?

All: We will.

Solo: Will you commit yourselves to responding to this voice in prayer and action?

All: We will.

Solo: Will you seek to dedicate your lives to the building up of God's kingdom, to making all things new?

All: We will.

Solo: As you long for God's Kingdom will you pray and act to renew the world marketplace so that the poorest have a better chance of life, and that all God's people might see an end to poverty?

All: By God's grace, we will.

Solo: Let us pray: We are small and insignificant, but trusting in God's grace let us take courage to pray:

**All: I dare to pray: Lord, let the world be changed, for I long to see the end of poverty;
I dare to pray: Lord, let the rules be changed for I long to see trade bring justice to the poor;
I dare to pray: Lord, let my life be changed, for I long to bring hope where good news is needed.**

In the strength of your Spirit and inspired by your compassion, I make this promise to work for change, and wait confidently for the day when you make all things new.

Amen.

Suggested songs for opening/closing worship

One bread, one body, one Lord of all	CG 98
For the fruits of all creation	CG 34 (tune CG 131)
The servant king	CG 128
We lay our broken world	CG 143
Longing for light	CG 21

SESSION FIVE:
EMPOWERMENT

But God chose what is foolish in the world to shame the wise; God chose what is weak in the world to shame the strong.

I Corinthians 1: 27

Looking Back and Introduction (5 minutes)

Welcome to the last study in the series. During the past four weeks, we have been called to a journey towards radical conversion. Firstly, we were challenged to turn to God and away from Mammon. Secondly, we were invited to use our talents and gifts for the service of others, rather than just for our own benefit. Thirdly, we were confronted by Christ's compassion towards the sick in contrast to the condemnation and exclusion by many of his contemporaries, especially by the leaders. Fourthly, we were reminded that God's justice demands protection for the weak and vulnerable and the abandoning of neutrality in the midst of injustice.

Today we are challenged to walk away from despair and from resignation. Though we are small and insignificant, with God's help we can make a difference. God is with us. We are called to work as if the establishment of God's reign depends on us and to pray as if everything depends on God.

Opening Worship (10 minutes)

Call to worship:
But God chose what is foolish in the world to shame the wise; God chose what is weak in the world to shame the strong;

(1 Corinthians 1: 27)

Prayers of Intercession:

Solo: Lord you placed us in the world to be its salt. Give us now your strength to confront the structures of injustice, the institutions, laws and practices that keep poor people disempowered. In your mercy,

All: **Lord, hear our prayer.**

Solo: Lord you placed us in the world to be its light. Give us now your strength to demand accountability, honesty and transparency in international law, governance, trade and aid.
In your mercy,

All: **Lord, hear our prayer.**

Solo: Lord you came to proclaim recovery of sight to the blind, to open the eyes of the oppressed and oppressors. Give us now your strength to work in solidarity with the poor and the courage to open our eyes to the injustices of our own lifestyles. In your mercy,

All: **Lord, hear our prayer.**

Solo: Lord you came to bring good news to the poor, to speak against injustice. Give us now the strength to support the oppressed as they speak out and challenge their rulers and the international community. In your mercy,

All: **Lord, hear our prayer.**

Solo: Lord you came to proclaim release to the captives and to set the oppressed free. Help us together, to break the chains that bind us, and transform them into a chain of solidarity.

All: **Amen.**

Let us pray:

We believe in the equality of all, rich and poor.
We believe in liberty.
We believe in the love within each of us,
and in the home, happy and healthy.
We believe in the forgiveness of our sins.
We believe that with divine help we will have the strength
to establish equality in society.
We believe in unity, the only way to achieve peace,
And we believe that together we can obtain justice.
Amen.

Explore (20 minutes)

On Super Heroes and Making a Difference

- As a group list on a sheet of paper (or flip-chart) what the attributes of a super–hero, like Batman or Superman, might be (eg great strength, X-ray vision, ability to fly).
- Now, on a separate sheet of paper, list the attributes which God has given to the ordinary people in your churches (or in your group).
- What characteristics do we need to have in order for us to be useful or valuable to God?

Reading and Listening (5 minutes)

God's Word

Call of a Prophet (Exodus 3: 1-12)

Moses was keeping the flock of his father-in-law Jethro, the priest of Midian; he led his flock beyond the wilderness, and came to Horeb, the mountain of God. There the angel of the Lord appeared to him in a flame of fire out of a bush; he looked, and the bush was blazing, yet it was not consumed …

Then the Lord said, 'I have observed the misery of my people who are in Egypt; I have heard their cry on account of their taskmasters. Indeed, I know their sufferings, and I have come down to deliver them from the Egyptians, and to bring them up out of that land to a good and broad land, a land flowing with milk and honey … The cry of the Israelites has now come to me; I have also seen how the Egyptians oppress them. So come, I will send you to Pharaoh to bring my people, the Israelites, out of Egypt.' But Moses said to God, 'Who am I that I should go to Pharaoh, and bring the Israelites out of Egypt?' He said, 'I will be with you; and this shall be the sign for you that it is I who sent you: when you have brought the people out of Egypt, you shall worship God on this mountain.'

(Matthew 21: 1-5)

When they had come near Jerusalem and had reached Bethphage, at the Mount of Olives, Jesus sent two disciples, saying to them, 'Go into the village ahead of you, and immediately you will find a donkey tied, and a colt with her; untie them and bring them to me. If anyone says anything to you, just say this, "The Lord needs them." And he will send them immediately.' This took place to fulfil what had been spoken through the prophet, saying, 'Tell the daughter of Zion, Look, your king is coming to you, humble, and mounted on a donkey, and on a colt, the foal of a donkey.'

Voice from the South

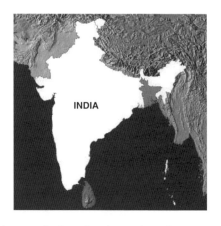

Indian Court Blocks Coca-Cola Water Supply (© the Guardian)

The income of many transnational corporations is bigger than those of the poorest countries of the world. It is not a surprise to hear stories of national governments evicting local populations to make way for foreign investments. Indigenous peoples are driven off their lands without adequate compensation and regarded as backward and obstacles to progress. Foreign investments are lured with offers of tax incentives and the national armies are utilised to provide security. With the coming together of economic, political and military forces, the poor are marginalized and excluded. Their protests fall on deaf ears. If they persist, the military can be used to silence them. News of repression is commonplace but a positive response to the poor's persistence is good news. It is a surprise.

Local residents in Kerala protested against the operation of the Coca-Cola plant. The company was making the people's shallow water pumps dry, turning their rice paddies into deserts and killing their coconut palms. But the state government supported the company. A thousand local families continued to protest for 20 months and brought out a legal action against Coca-Cola in defiance of the state government. The court ruled in favour of the local residents. In turn, Coca-Cola was ordered to close its boreholes and stop drawing ground water in a month's time because it was ruining the environment.

The court ruled that extraction of the ground water at Plachimada village, even up to the limit admitted by the company, was illegal. The company had no right to extract this much natural wealth and the panchayat (local authority) and the government were bound to prevent it. The court argued that groundwater was a national resource that belonged to the entire society. It was not right for the company to use so much water to keep the plant in operation because it deprived the local population of the water they needed in order to survive.

'Ground water under the land of the company does not belong to it,' said Justice K Balakrishnan Nair. 'Every landowner can draw a "reasonable" amount of ground water that is necessary for its domestic and agricultural requirements. But here, 510,000 litres of water is extracted per day, converted to products and transported, thus breaking the natural water cycle.'

Discussion (30 minutes)

All the great prophets hesitated in accepting God's call because they were aware of their frailties and weaknesses. Moses was not an exception.

When Jesus made his triumphal entry into Jerusalem, he didn't ride a chariot or a warhorse. He sat on a donkey. He didn't ascend a throne but was lifted up on a cross five days later. And today he re-lives his passion and death in the lives of the 'little ones'. What we do or do not do to the least of our brothers and sisters, we are doing to him. (Matthew 25: 45) But the journey does not finish with death. There is resurrection. There is hope.

a. Can you think of other examples from the Bible (or more recent figures) when God unexpectedly chose the small, weak or 'foolish' to achieve his purpose, and for his glory?
b. What does God say to encourage Moses, and to encourage us?
c. What relevance does the passage from Exodus have to the experience of the people from Kerala?
d. There are people who kill or die for love of money and power. What message is proclaimed through the symbolism of riding a donkey and dying on the cross?

Reflection (10 minutes)

One day a young man felt alone and lonely. He looked and stared at his fingerprints. Time passed and gradually loneliness gave way to apprehension and excitement. He wrote:

> No one has lived, no one is alive,
> and no one will ever live with your fingerprints.
>
> There is a love that only your heart can give;
>   a kind word that only your tongue can utter;
>   a welcoming smile that only your lips can offer;
>   a task that only your hands can do;
>   a journey that only your feet can make.
> If you refuse to do any of these, it is forever left undone.
>
> You are unique.
> God loves you with a love that's meant only for you.
> But with uniqueness and love, come responsibility.
> This is the message of your fingerprints.
>
>   Romy Tiongco

We need to move on. Let us open our hearts to God's presence and offer ourselves to the Lord. Let us stay silent for a few moments and listen to our need for God.

Closing Worship (10 minutes)

Call to worship: Do not be afraid of them, for I am with you to deliver you.

                                                   (Jeremiah 1: 8)

Leader: God invites us to continue Jesus' mission to proclaim that the 'Reign of God is here'. God knows our weaknesses and frailties. Like the prophets we must learn to rely on the promise: 'I will be with you.'

The response is: **Your kingdom come!**

Voice 1: For I am about to create new heavens and a new earth; the former things shall not be remembered or come to mind. No more shall the sound of weeping be heard in it, or the cry of distress. Lord, we pray:

All: **Your kingdom come!**

Voice 2: No more shall there be in it an infant that lives but a few days, or an old person who does not live out a lifetime; for one who dies at a hundred years will be considered a youth. Lord, we pray:

All: **Your kingdom come!**

Voice 3: They shall build houses and inhabit them; they shall plant vineyards and eat their fruit. They shall not build and another inhabit; they shall not plant and another eat; for like the days of a tree shall the days of my people be, and my chosen shall long enjoy the work of their hands. Lord, we pray:

All: **Your kingdom come!**

Voice 4: They shall not labour in vain, or bear children for calamity; for they shall be offspring blessed by the Lord - and their descendants as well. Before they call I will answer, while they are yet speaking I will hear. Lord, we pray:

All: **Your kingdom come!**

Voice 5: The wolf and the lamb shall feed together, the lion shall eat straw like the ox; but the serpent - its food shall be dust! They shall not hurt or destroy on all my holy mountain. Lord, we pray:

All: **Your kingdom come!**

Let us pray together the Lord's Prayer:
Our Father ...

Suggested songs for opening/closing worship:

Give me the faith which can remove	MP 168
God of grace and God of glory	CH3 88
Be still, for the presence of the Lord	CG 12 MP 50
Spirit of the living God	CG 116 MP 613

Notes for Facilitators

Making the most of 'Voices from the South'

It is hoped that the group sessions from Voices from the South will provide a reflective, encouraging and prayerful experience for all who take part in them. To enable the sessions to run as effectively as possible, all participants are encouraged to share in their preparation and facilitation. It may be helpful to agree for different people to look after different aspects of each session - from chairs to prayers. It is highly recommended that the facilitation of the formal part of the session be shared by two people working closely together as a team.

1. About being facilitators

General tips
The role of the facilitators is to help the session to run smoothly and to allow the experience to be as positive as possible. They have the main responsibility for creating the atmosphere for the session. This will include setting up a comfortable and welcoming space and establishing a sense of trust, mutual respect and sharing among the participants. The facilitators also have to try to keep the session to its agreed topic and time.
They should try to encourage aspects such as respect, dialogue, listening, exploration and the sharing of experience, understanding, belief, insight and story. They should try to avoid aspects such as debate, argument, intellectualisation, wandering off the topic or letting any one person dominate the group (including the facilitators themselves!).
Facilitators have to put more effort into asking key questions and listening to people's responses rather than talking themselves. Think in terms of inviting, but not forcing, others to share a response. Good questions are 'open' questions, like, 'Who? Why? What? How?...do you think/feel?' These allow people to tap into and share their own experience and understanding. One useful technique for encouraging each person to share something is to break into groups of three (two or four can also work). Ask the threes to buzz for a few minutes on the question and then invite a little feedback from each of the small groups to the full group. This should be more like a 'flavour', rather than a 'summary', of what has been said. Particular points may then be explored further as a full group. (Breaking into threes can also be helpful if any one person is tending to dominate the full group.) Following a rhythm of reflecting alone, sharing in threes and exploring in

the full group will often help the session reach deeper and more satisfying places. Working with another facilitator makes it much easier to manage all this. Agree between you who will be responsible for which question or part of the session.

Before the session
Be as familiar as possible with the venue. Check the 'ordinary' things that are so important: that the room is comfortable and welcoming; that there are enough chairs; that the biscuits are ready.
Be as familiar as possible with the session, the topic and the material. If required, prepare photocopies or check that the CD is at the right track. Many people create a centrepiece to help establish a visual focus which can help support this kind of reflection. The centrepiece may contain items such as a Bible, candle, coloured cloth, flowers or icon. Try to keep it simple and tasteful. You may find it helpful to have a world map or globe to hand, for looking up where the stories from 'the South' come from. Some of these tasks may be taken on by other members of the group.

At the start of the session
It helps at the start of a series of meetings to let everyone introduce themselves and to repeat this at later sessions if someone new comes along. Make sure that everyone knows how long the session is likely to last. Make a clear start to the formal part of the session. Remind everyone of the invitation to share and to share only what is comfortable and appropriate in this group. Avoid giving too long an introduction.

During the session
Have an idea of when you expect people to be reflecting quietly on their own, working in threes or working in the full group.
Keep looking around the group, being sensitive to people's body language. Encourage and invite them to contribute. Not everyone is comfortable speaking out loud in a group, but no matter how silent someone may appear, they will be reflecting on what is going on. Remember that not everyone is comfortable with reading aloud.

After the session
Confirm details for the next meeting and who will be taking responsibility for different parts of the preparation. Thank everyone for their participation. And finally... Be creative in your facilitating. You bring plenty of your own skills and experience. Use them. Relax and enjoy this valuable service.

2. Aims and key objectives for the Sessions

Session 1: Poverty

Aim: To realise that the problem of poverty is a problem of wealth with deep religious significance, and understand that our happiness is with God, not earthly possessions
- to recognise and face our longing for God
- to value times of quiet and being alone
- to recognise and rejoice in God's liberating presence in the struggles of ordinary people

Session 2: Education

Aim: To value education as a human right but also as a privilege and a gift that, along with our other talents and gifts, is for sharing and using to serve God and our neighbours
- to realise that there are people who still do not have access to good education
- to appreciate the dedication of the 'Ernas' of this world to get an education
- to encourage a desire to support institutions and organisations providing education to the poor

Session 3: Health

Aim: To encounter the compassionate God and understand that our relationship with those 'less fortunate' than us should be based on compassion, not condemnation
- to confront our attitude towards HIV/AIDS
- to encounter the compassion of Jesus

Session 4: Trade

Aim: To encounter God's understanding of justice, his preferential option for the vulnerable
- to adopt the Biblical understanding of justice that is biased towards the poor, weak, oppressed and marginalized
- to understand that there is a moral argument for the Trade Justice campaign
- to generate enthusiasm to participate in campaign actions
- to challenge us to buy fairly traded products as a way of sharing earthly wealth

Session 5: Empowerment

Aim: To understand salvation as total liberation and see that all Christians have a role to play in God's kingdom on earth

- to understand that the call to advocacy and campaign is based on the realisation that, though we are small, we can make a difference
- to integrate life and faith, living and believing
- to accept our part in proclaiming God's reign
- to continue to pray that God's kingdom come!

3. Notes and instructions

Timing

Each session offers material designed to last about 90 minutes, and suggested timings have been given for each section. If you want your study session to last longer, there is the opportunity to spend more time on certain parts of the session.

Welcome and looking back

Apart from session one, each session opens with a chance to recall the previous group meeting. This will set the context for beginning the new study.

Worship

Each session includes suggestions for opening and closing worship, usually prayers, but you can of course devise your own worship material and encourage open prayer, silent reflection and so on.

No specific place for songs is given during the main body of notes for each session, but the suggested timings allow for including this important element of worship if you want to. You will find suggestions for hymns and worship songs at the end of each session. They can be found in the following books, as well as in many other widely used hymn books:

- Common Ground (CG) - 'a song book for all the churches', published by The Saint Andrew Press
- Mission Praise (MP) - published by Marshall Pickering
- The Church Hymnary, Third Edition, (CH3) published by Oxford University Press

Reading out loud

There are many opportunities for group members to participate. Wherever possible ask different people to read scripture passages, stories, poems, prayers. You may like to forewarn people, so that they have a chance to familiarise themselves with the material.

Moving forward

This section appears towards the end of each session. It is an opportunity for summing up what people have experienced/ learned, and for considering what they might take away with them for further thought, reflection, prayer or practical action.

Session 1

Explore: The Step Forward Game

For this group exercise you will need to allocate to each group member one of the "characters" from the following list of situations:

1. Drug user HIV+. Refused housing association housing because of drug use.
2. Pregnant 17-year-old living in bed and breakfast accommodation.
3. Owner-occupier on good steady income.
4. Member of a family living in good quality council accommodation.
5. Newly qualified graduate, unemployed, with large student loan to repay.
6. One of an elderly couple living in large owner-occupied house in need of repair.
7. Man living in private rented flat. The owner wants to put up the rent, which you cannot afford to pay.
8. One of a family of asylum seekers living on inner-city council estate facing racial harassment.
9. Young woman, aged 16, has left home and moved to London to escape abuse. Has spent the last few nights living on the street.
10. Elderly man leaving psychiatric hospital to move into the 'community'.
11. One of the parents of a young family who cannot make mortgage repayments and are threatened with repossession.
12. Student living in university hall of residence.

Paper alternative

If the space you have is limited, or people prefer to remain seated, you may like to consider the following paper alternative:

- Allocate each member of the group one of the characters from the above list
- Give each person a pen and paper, and ask them the questions, on page 14.
- If, as the character in their given situation, they can answer "yes", they can score 2 points, if "no" they score no points.
- At the end of the questions each person reveals how many points they have, and then the group continues with the discussion, as indicated in Session 1.

Session 3

This session focuses on the health and development issue of HIV/AIDS. For a different approach to health and disability which challenges us to see disability as a gift, see the paper, "A church of all and for all: an interim statement" prepared for the central committee of the World Council of Churches meeting August - September 2003. It can be found on the World Council of Churches website: www.wcc-coe.org

Session 4

Explore: Quiz

Answers: 1.c) 2.c) 3.b) 4.a) 5.c) 6.c) 7.c) 8.b) 9.b) 10.c)

4. Additional Resources

- Material based on this study guide and suitable for use with children and young people can be found on the ACTS website: www.acts-scotland.org
- A list of additional resource materials and websites for further study of the Millennium Development Goals and the themes of poverty, development and trade can be found on the ACTS website: www.acts-scotland.org

5. Evaluation

We would be grateful if you could complete and return the evaluation questionnaire to be found on the ACTS website. This will help us with the production of future study material. Thank you.

Acknowledgements

ACTS and CTBI gratefully acknowledge permission to reproduce copyright material in this publication. Every effort has been made to trace and contact copyright holders. The publishers will gladly rectify any error or omission in future editions.

Text and notes of The New English Bible © the delegates of the Oxford University Press and the Syndics of the Cambridge University Press, 1961, 1970.

In addition we acknowledge:

Session 1:
• Opening worship adapted from a piece by Joe Seremane, South Africa Lifelines (Christian Aid 1987).
• Explore: the 'Step Forward Game' is adapted from an exercise in *Windows and Walls* – A housing action handbook for churches published by Church Action on Poverty, 1991.
• Voice from the South: *An economy based on solidarity* – adapted from Judith Escribano's slide presentation for Christian Aid Week (CAW) 2003.
• Moving Forward: Poem, *If the hunger of others* by Javier Torres, Nicaragua, Continent of Hope, CAFOD, 1992, from Solidarity with the people of Nicaragua, published by Orbis Books.
• Closing worship: Prayer of Confession and Thanksgiving, Companion to the Revised Common Lectionary Vol.2 All Age Worship Year A, by Julie M Hulme 1998. Used by permission of the Methodist Publishing House.

Session 2:
• Introduction: Quotation from Handbook, *Training for Transformation*, Book IV by Anne Hope and Sally Timmel, published by ITDG
• Voice from the South: *Erna's story* provided by Myrna Bajo.
• Opening worship: Prayer of Acknowledgement, Companion to the Revised Common Lectionary Vol. 2 All Age Worship Year A © Julie M Hulme, 1998. Used by permission of the Methodist Publishing House.

Session 3:
• Opening worship: some lines from Prayer of Confession, Companion to the Revised Common Lectionary Vol.2 All Age Worship Year A, by Julie M Hulme, 1998. Used by permission of the Methodist Publishing House.
• Explore: The diagram is taken from the "m: power" booklet, published by Christian Aid. It first appeared in *Youth Topics the ultimate collection* by Catherine Kash, produced by CAFOD, Christian Aid and SCIAF.
• Voice from the South: *Julie's story* is from *Picturing Life with HIV/AIDS* published by Christian Aid.
• Moving Forward: statistics from UNAIDS website (2003).
• Closing worship: material taken from:
Paragraph one is from *AIDS: Sharing the Pain*, Bill Kirkpatrick 1998. Published by Darton Longman and Todd.
Voice 2, *We give you thanks..* is adapted from *Anthology and Suggestions for Worship, World AIDS day 1991*, CTBI
Voice 2, *Lord may we go..* is from *An Ecumenical Service of Hope and Remembrance to mark World AIDS Day 1995, Southwark Cathedral*, London Ecumenical AIDS Trust
Voice 1 quotes are from *AIDS and the African churches: exploring the challenges*, by Gillian Paterson, Christian Aid 2001.
Final Prayer: *From Shore to Shore: Liturgies, Litanies and Prayers From Around the World.* by USPG, 2003. Editor Kate Wyles, Published by SPCK.

Session 4:
• Opening worship: *God of the just weight..* is from Honduras, author and source unknown, taken from page 32 of *Prayers, poems, songs and reflections from Latin America and the Caribbean*, complied in 2002 by Judith Escribano, published by Christian Aid.
• Voice from the South: *Meiri's story* – adapted from CAW 2002 Ghana report by Louise Orston and Mary Bradford
• Closing worship – the *"I dare to pray"* (the Trade Pledge prayer) is from Trade for Life Worship and Study Guide, © Peter Graystone / Christian Aid.

Session 5:
• Opening worship: *I believe in the equality of all*, by an Ayacucho youth group in Peru, from *Celebrating one World*, editors Linda Jones / Bernadette Farrell / Annabel Shilson-Thomas. CAFOD / Harper Collins 1998.
• Voice from the South: *Indian Court Blocks Coca-Cola Water supply* – article by Paul Brown from The Guardian, 19 December 2003 © The Guardian.

Thanks are due to:
• Helen Hood and Nikki Macdonald for ideas for group exercises.
• Brother Stephen Smyth for contributions to the facilitators' notes.
• The study groups in Eastwood, Motherwell, Troon, Edinburgh, Granton, Musselburgh, Aberdeen, Broughty Ferry, Wishaw, Pollokshaws, Bathgate, Atholl, Iona, Rosyth, Kilmarnock, Paisley, Bishopbriggs, Longniddry, Perth, Lochearnhead, Edzell and Queensferry who piloted the material, and whose comments and suggestions were so helpful.
• The ecumenical team from ACTS who made this project possible.